This book property of

M.F. OBERLENDER

B270   Animalia by Graeme Base   © Harry N. Abrams, Inc. 1986

PIE

A Guessing Game of Sayings

by Marcia and Michael Folsom

Pictures by Jack Kent

Clarion Books

TICKNOR & FIELDS: A HOUGHTON MIFFLIN COMPANY

New York

For Jamie and Raphael
With your fresh thoughts

Clarion Books
Ticknor & Fields, a Houghton Mifflin Company

Text copyright© 1985 by Marcia and Michael Folsom
Illustrations copyright © 1985 by Jack Kent

Library of Congress Cataloging in Publication Data
Folsom, Michael.
  Easy as pie.

  Summary: Introduces the letters of the alphabet with
such familiar sayings as A—Straight as an arrow, B—
Snug as a bug in a rug.
  [1. Alphabet] I. Folsom, Marcia McClintock.
II. Kent, Jack, 1920-   ill. III. Title.
PZ7.F73563Eas 1985 [E] 84-14978
ISBN 0-89919-303-X

H 10 9 8 7 6 5 4 3 2

A

Straight as an

Arrow

Snug as a

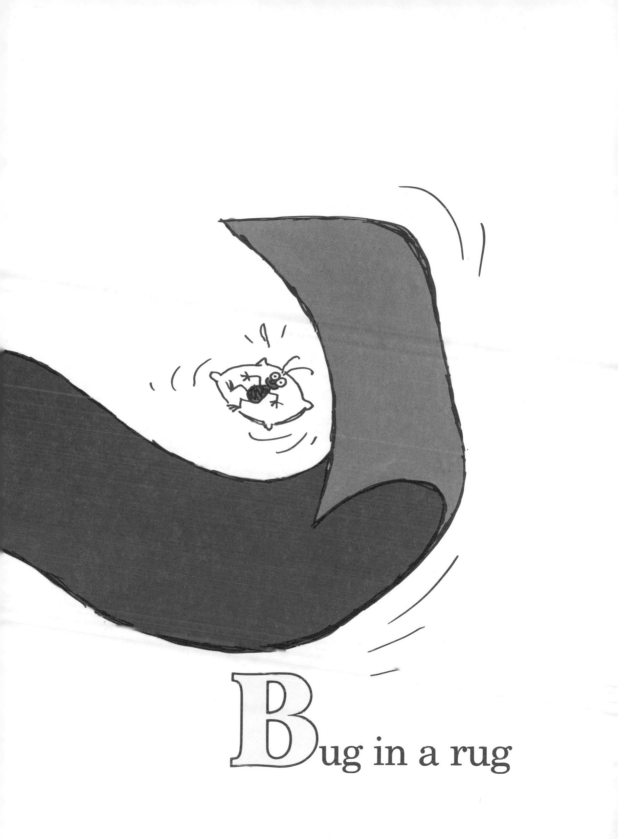

Bug in a rug

C

Cool as a

Cucumber

D

Dark as a

Dungeon

E

Slippery as an

Eel

F

Sly as a

Fox

G

Silly as a

Goose

H

Mad as a

wet **H**en

I

Cold as

Ice

J

Noisy as a

Jay

K

High as a

Kite

L

Crazy as a

Stubborn as a

N

Tough as

Nails

O

Strong as an

Ox

P

Flat as a

Pancake

Plump as a

Quail

R

Sweet as a

Rose

Deep as the

Sea

T

Warm as

Rare as a

Unicorn

Shy as a

Violet

W

Clean as a

Whistle

X

Merry as

Xmas

Y

Wide as a

Yawn

Stuck as a

Zipper

Easy as Pie

Playing with Sayings
–Old and New

He walked like a slow frog, and he was dressed in an astronaut's suit with a fish tank on his head! That is how our son Jamie described an exterminator who had come to get rid of a wasps' nest in his second grade classroom. We could visualize this bizarre apparition more clearly because of Jamie's vivid analogies. Children as well as adults use many kinds of comparisons in speech. They seem to learn the art naturally, as an extension of description.

Children also inherit many comparisons in the form of old sayings like "wise as an owl," "light as a feather," and "old as the hills." For adults, such expressions are clichés, not inventions, and we pass them along without seeing their images. For children, however, old sayings are new when they first hear them. Playing with these old sayings often inspires children to make up funny, rude, or fantastic coinages of their own.

Most of the twenty-seven phrases in our book are "old sayings," and give children the pleasure of either recognizing them or adding them to their repertoire. Like those in this book, some of the most familiar old sayings are comparisons that capture a resemblance to an animal or a bird: "quick as a rabbit," "cold as a fish," "proud as a peacock." Others are based on simple manufactured or natural objects: "sharp as a tack," "thin as a reed," "plain as the nose on your face." Still others use the weather as a source for comparisons: "quick as lightning," "right as rain," "white as snow."

Some old sayings are simply common sense and their origins are easily guessed, as in "slow as a turtle." Others, though now clichés, seem very inventive: "happy as a clam." There are also comparisons people use without knowing their obscure original meanings: "mad as a hatter," for instance. Mercury, which formerly was used in processing felt, poisoned hat-makers and caused their minds to deteriorate.

A few old sayings are mysteriously idiomatic, like the title of this book: why, indeed, is pie "easy"?

Our book is intended for children who have already mastered the alphabet, but enjoy reciting it, and are ready to learn more complex verbal formulas. Using their own memories and the visual clues provided by Jack Kent's illustrations, they will be able to guess the missing words in most of these comparisons. Then they can make up "old" sayings of their own. Some will enjoy thinking up nonsense comparisons: "thin as a mouse," "friendly as a pancake," "angry as an onion." Often children will come up with fresh, accurate new analogies. Our son Raphael suggested one of the comparisons we use in this book: "plump as a quail," which seems so apt it almost deserves to be an old saying.

When children get the hang of it, making up such verbal inventions is easy as pie.

—*The Authors*